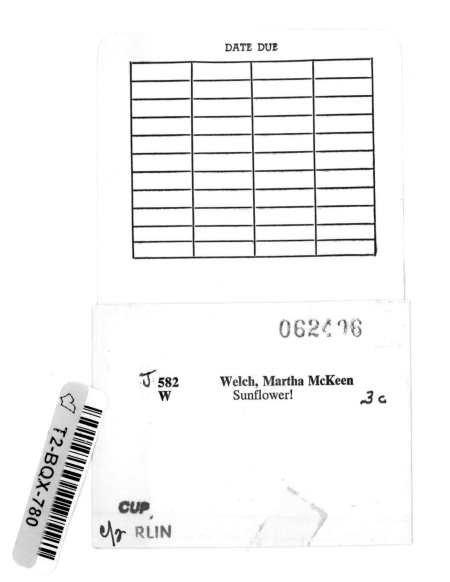

DATE DUE

MARTHA McKEEN WELCH

SUNFLOWER!

DODD, MEAD & COMPANY
NEW YORK

For reviewing the text and photographs of this book the author would
like to thank Mary-Ann Karpel, Ph.D., Consulting Entomologist, Brooklyn
Botanic Gardens; Silas S. Hagar, Ph.D., Research Plant Pathologist,
Brooklyn Botanic Gardens; Jean Craighead George, Author, Natural-
ist. Special thanks to Peter R. Limburg for his inspiration.

01 B5142

1 2 3 4 5 6 7 8 9 10

Library of Congress Cataloging in Publication Data

Welch, Martha McKeen.
Sunflower!

SUMMARY: Text and photographs chronicle
the growth of a sunflower seed into a tall,
stately flower.
1.   Sunflowers — Juvenile literature.
[1.   Sunflowers]   I.   Title.
QK495.C74W38   583'.55   80-1008
ISBN 0-396-07885-0

For Ellen Lea Chidsey, with love

What made that hole in the sunflower leaf?

A daddy longlegs?

No. It is just resting its eight long legs on the sunflower
plant. Like its cousin the spider, the daddy longlegs eats
insects, not sunflower leaves. But it can't spin a web.

A walkingstick?

No. It is just walking on the sunflower plant. A walking-stick prefers to eat leaves on trees. When it stands still, it looks like a twig or part of a leaf, so its enemies cannot easily spot it.

A scarab beetle?

Could be! It eats lots of holes in sunflower leaves. It also eats holes in sunflower petals.

What else happens to a sunflower plant?

A sunflower plant can grow so tall that you need a ladder to reach the sunflower at the top.

The sunflower might be as big as your head. Or even bigger. It is called the flower head.

Or, it might be as small as this one growing out of a
hole in the tree. Its long thin stem is not strong enough to
hold the sunflower up. To grow tall and strong, a sunflower plant needs rich soil and lots of sun and water.

Where does a sunflower plant come from? What makes it grow?

A sunflower plant comes from a sunflower seed. Compare the seeds to the size of a penny. The seed coats all look a little different, but inside they are all alike.

What's inside? Let's watch a seed grow and find out.

To start growing, a seed needs water. A blotter can be
put in a glass with some water in the bottom. A sunflower
seed can be placed between the side of the glass and
the blotter. The blotter will absorb water and keep the
seed wet. The seed will start to grow, just as though we
planted it in the ground. But now we can watch it.

It has started! Something white is coming out of the seed!

After three or four days, a tiny root tip pushes out. As it grows, it turns down. Root hairs begin to sprout. The stem and seed grow up.

In another day or two, the roots are longer. More have sprouted. Now they need warm, rich soil. They will suck up water and nourishment from the soil so that the plant can grow big and healthy. They will hold the sunflower plant tightly in the ground. A plant cannot grow without roots. The stem is growing, too.

Time to transplant the delicate sprouting seed to a flower pot. It is placed gently in the soil and covered with a little more soil. Then it is watered.

Here comes the stem, pushing right through the dirt in the pot! The small tender stem pushes up and straightens out, all in a single day. It is strong for its size.

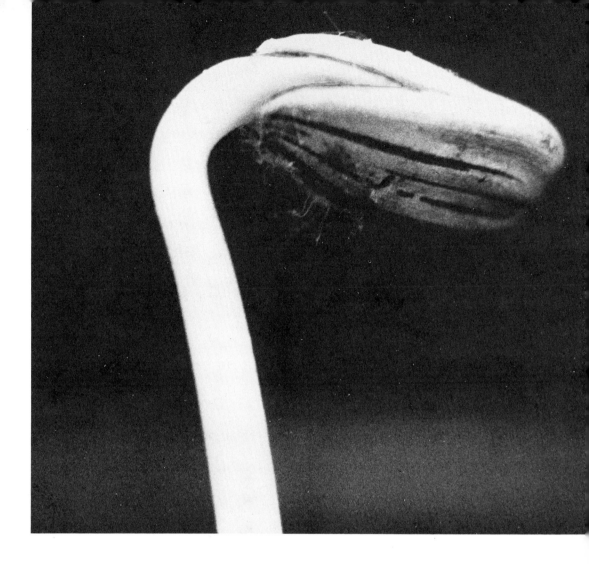

The seed coat is still on top. What's inside the seed coat?

Two plump little leaves called seed leaves are inside
the seed coat. As the stem grows, the seed leaves grow,
too. They turn from white to green in the sun and wear
the seed coat like a hat.

Oops! The hat fell off!

The seed leaves spread apart and made the seed coat fall off. Seed leaves have enough food stored in them to help the plant grow other leaves. The new sunflower leaves sprout between the seed leaves. Can you see them?

More and more leaves appear: two, four, six, eight, up and up. The new leaves can make food inside themselves using sunlight, air, and water from the earth. The seed leaves will dry up and fall off when they are no longer needed.

The sunflower plant has grown. Time to move it to the garden.

What's that worm doing?

Eating dirt! It digests tiny bits of dead plants, insects, and other things in the dirt. The waste matter passes through the worm's body back into the soil, making the soil richer. The tunnels the worm makes in the ground let water and air get to the roots of the sunflower plant. Just by the way it lives, the worm helps the sunflower plant grow.

Look what a thunderstorm did to the sunflower plant!
Will it die?

No. The stem is only bent, not broken. Moisture can still travel up inside the stem from the roots. In two days, it has straightened up.

Eight weeks pass. The sun-flower plant is about as tall as it will grow.

A small bud forms at the top. It is the same color as the
leaves. Can you find it?

As the bud gets bigger, it is easy to see. It has pointed green petals called bracts. They protect what is growing inside.

What is growing inside?

When the bracts open, there is a circle of yellow sun-flower petals underneath. These are ray petals. Their bright color attracts insects. Soon they start to open, too.
Is there more inside?

When the yellow ray petals open, there are hundreds
more little buds inside. They are all tucked together in a
pretty pattern on a flat circle called a disk. Soon there
will be hundreds of little flowers.

The sunflower head is called a composite flower. A composite flower has many little flowers put together to look like one big flower.

The buds start to open from the outside of the disk toward the center. The flowers are called florets.

Each floret contains a pistil, which has three parts: the stigma, the style, and the ovary. The stigma stands up above the opening petals. It is at the top of the style, which connects it to the ovary at the base of the pistil. Each floret also has a stamen with yellow pollen on it. These small parts are very important to the sunflower plant.

The disk keeps growing to make room for more florets
to open. Insects come and go all day.

They suck sweet juice called nectar from deep inside the florets. Bees take nectar home to make honey.

Insects get the pollen from the stamens all over themselves. As they move around, they bump into the sticky stigmas and get some pollen grains on them, too. A pollen grain makes a tube down inside the style to the ovary. Then something important starts to happen.

What starts to happen? Wait and see.

An orange fritillary butterfly zooms in. It likes to suck sweet nectar, too. Will the bees sting it?

No. They are not interested. They just move over to make room for the butterfly.

Many kinds of insects visit the sunflower plant. Squash
bugs come.

Katydids come. They jump all around the plant using their strong hind legs.

All sorts of beetles come. Some suck juice from the leaves and stems. Some suck nectar from inside the florets. Some help the sunflower plant by killing insects that harm it.

Tiny, shiny flies come.
They sparkle many colors in
the sun.

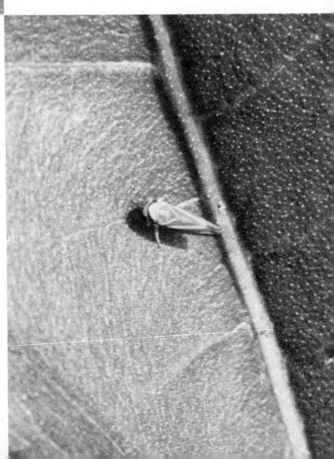

Little bright-colored leaf-
hoppers come. They hop
hop hop all around.

Teeny whiteflies come. Sometimes there are so many
on the underside of a leaf that if you shake it, they fly up
like a white cloud. Whiteflies can suck so much juice that
a leaf may turn brown and die.

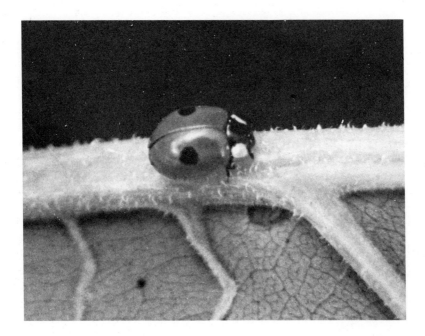

Here comes a ladybird beetle. It eats many small insects that hurt the plant. It lays eggs on the underside of
the leaves. Its babies eat harmful insects, too.

A spider comes to the leaf to spin a shelter for her egg ball. She makes a round white waterproof ball that contains her eggs. Then she covers it over with a web. During the winter, the leaf will die, mother spider will die, but the egg ball will be safe. Baby spiders will hatch out in the spring.

Watching a sunflower plant is better than going to the zoo!

A big sunflower plant gets very heavy. The main stem has to be thick and strong.

All the stems are quite wet inside. If one is damaged, moisture will come out in big drops until the stem heals.

Another month passes. Days are shorter. Nights are cooler. Fall is coming. The flower head droops.

The yellow ray petals fall off. The bracts are still there to protect the disk. What have the florets been doing all this time?

Look closely. A few florets have fallen off. What do you see?

Sunflower seeds! The florets have been making new seeds! From just one seed that was planted, there are now hundreds of brand new seeds.

Each floret has done a wonderful thing. The roots have helped. The stems have helped. The leaves have helped. Insects have helped. Many things have helped the florets make new sunflower seeds.

When the florets drop off, the new seeds will be just like the one that was planted.

Autumn is here. The leaves get moldy.

The roots loosen in the ground. The whole sun-flower plant withers and dies.

Down it falls in a great big mess. Worms, bacteria, mold, ants, and many other creatures start eating the dead plant. In a few years, when it has all decayed, the sunflower plant will be part of the soil. There will be no trace of it left.

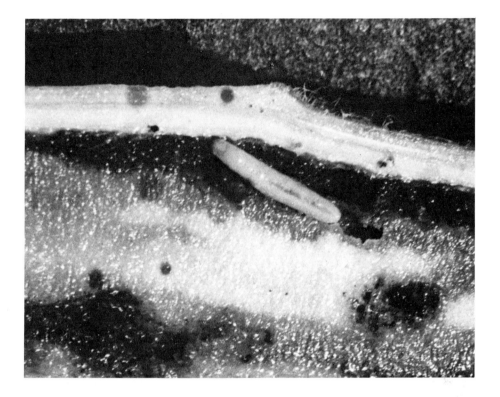

What is that thing inside the broken stem? It is moving!

A larva. It hatched from an egg laid on the outside of the stem. Then it ate its way inside. There it had a safe place with lots of food where no birds could eat it. The larva will change inside the stem during the winter and fly away as a moth in spring. Even when a sunflower plant is dead, it can be used for shelter.

But what happens to the seeds?

Sometimes seeds scatter all over the ground.

Sometimes birds pick out all the seeds, every single
one, before the plant falls over.

Most often, the flower head is saved. Sunflower seeds
can be used in many ways: as food for people and
livestock,

for birds in winter,

for other animal friends, and

for you to plant in the ground next spring.

Martha McKeen Welch has been interested in nature for most of her life. Growing up in Easton, Pennsylvania, she had all kinds of pets: dogs, cats, monkeys, ponies, a coatimundi, and even a raccoon that sometimes slept in bed with her. She studied in France and graduated from art school in San Francisco and New York City, where she also studied photography and ran her own design studio. Her work has appeared in numerous publications and exhibits. She has traveled in forty-seven states, all over Europe, and in India, Nepal, Mexico, and North Africa, always taking pictures. In addition to raising her own family (two children, now grown), she has raised dogs, cats, birds, mice, and even a family of bush babies. She lives with her husband in Mount Kisco, New York. Among her previous books for children are *Pudding and Pie* and *Saucy.*